12 QUESTIONS ABOUT THE
GETTYSBURG ADDRESS

by Mirella S. Miller

12 STORY LIBRARY

www.12StoryLibrary.com

12-Story Library is an imprint of Peterson Publishing Company and Press Room Editions.

Produced for 12-Story Library by Red Line Editorial

Photographs ©: Everett Historical/Shutterstock Images, cover, 1, 5, 12, 28; Library of Congress, 4, 9, 13, 16, 20, 25, 29; Corbis, 6, 21; lillisphotography/iStockphoto, 7; Photopa1/iStock/Thinkstock, 8; Nancy Honeycutt/iStockphoto, 10; Delmas Lehman/Shutterstock Images, 11; Michael Poe/iStock/ Thinkstock, 14; gnagel/iStockphoto, 15; Susan Law Cain/iStock/Thinkstock, 17; AdamParent/iStock/ Thinkstock, 18; Fansher/iStock/Thinkstock, 19; AP Images, 22, 27; PhotosByPaulReitmeir/iStock/ Thinkstock, 23; billnoll/iStockphoto, 24; Joe Gough/Shutterstock Images, 26

Library of Congress Cataloging-in-Publication Data
Names: Miller, Mirella S., author.
Title: 12 questions about the Gettysburg Address / by Mirella S. Miller.
Other titles: Twelve questions about the Gettysburg Address
Description: Mankato, MN : 12-Story Library, 2017. | Series: Examining
   primary sources | Includes bibliographical references and index. |
   Audience: Grades 4-6.
Identifiers: LCCN 2016002338 (print) | LCCN 2016002594 (ebook) | ISBN
   9781632352842 (library bound : alk. paper) | ISBN 9781632353344 (pbk. :
   alk. paper) | ISBN 9781621434511 (hosted ebook)
Subjects: LCSH: Lincoln, Abraham, 1809-1865. Gettysburg address--Juvenile
   literature. | United States--History--Civil War, 1861-1865--Juvenile
   literature.
Classification: LCC E475.55 .M64 2016 (print) | LCC E475.55 (ebook) | DDC
   973.7/349--dc23
LC record available at http://lccn.loc.gov/2016002338

Printed in the United States of America
Mankato, MN
May, 2016

Access free, up-to-date content on this topic plus a full digital version of this book. Scan the QR code on page 31 or use your school's login at 12StoryLibrary.com.

Table of Contents

What Events Led to the Gettysburg Address?

The United States was a divided country in the mid-1800s. The North and the South could not agree on the issue of slavery. Some people believed the government should not decide if slavery was legal in new territories. But Abraham Lincoln became president in 1861, and he did not support slavery. Upset by this, 11 states in the South left the United States. They formed the Confederate

GO TO THE SOURCE

To read the full text of the Gettysburg Address, go to **www.12StoryLibrary.com/primary**.

States of America in 1861. Soon, Confederate troops were fighting troops from the Union. Union states still belonged to the United States.

The US Civil War would continue until 1865. However, the worst battle

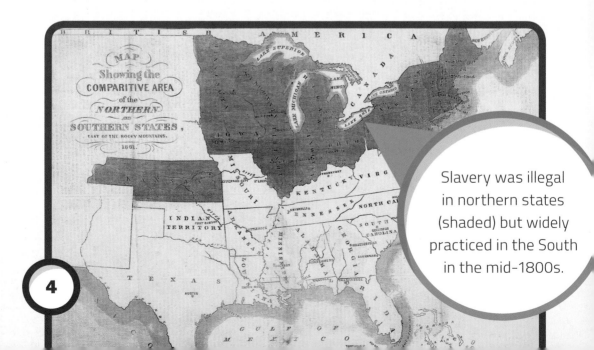

Slavery was illegal in northern states (shaded) but widely practiced in the South in the mid–1800s.

THE NORTH VS. THE SOUTH

The North and the South had different climates and industries. The North had many factories. There were some small farms, too. The South had many large farms. It took a lot of workers to run these farms, also called plantations. Plantation owners enslaved other humans to work on their farms. Most enslaved people were treated harshly. They worked long hours and were not paid for their work. Making slavery illegal meant plantation owners would lose their free help.

happened in July 1863. The Battle of Gettysburg lasted three days. Confederate troops had advanced to Gettysburg, Pennsylvania. Union soldiers attacked. After days of fighting, the Union won the battle.

More than 165,000 soldiers fought in the Battle of Gettysburg. Some reports estimate that nearly 10,000 of these soldiers died on the battlefield. They needed to be buried somewhere. Judge David Wills from Pennsylvania suggested creating a national cemetery at Gettysburg. Wills believed a dedication should take place once the cemetery was ready. He invited President Lincoln to speak at the ceremony.

51,000
Estimated number of soldiers killed, injured, or missing after the Battle of Gettysburg.

- The North and the South had different views on slavery.
- Eleven southern states formed the Confederate States of America.
- The US Civil War lasted until 1865.
- The Battle of Gettysburg was the deadliest battle of the war.

The Battle of Gettysburg was the deadliest of all battles in the US Civil War.

5

What Is the Gettysburg Address?

Several people spoke at the dedication of the Gettysburg National Cemetery on November 19, 1863. But one stood out. President Lincoln was not the main speaker of the event. Former Massachusetts governor Edward Everett delivered the keynote speech. But Lincoln's remarks, which later became known as the Gettysburg Address, have been discussed ever since.

Lincoln kept his address short the day of the ceremony. Judge Wills had only asked for a few remarks from the president. Lincoln wanted to honor the Union soldiers who had died during the Battle of Gettysburg in his speech. He also wanted to assure the crowd that the nation would move forward after the war. Lincoln knew this was a difficult time for the nation. He did not want Americans to give up hope.

Everett was a well-known speaker and had run for vice president in 1860.

54

Lincoln's age when he delivered the Gettysburg Address.

- Lincoln was not the main speaker of the dedication ceremony.
- His speech came to be referred to as the Gettysburg Address.
- Lincoln kept his speech short.
- The Gettysburg Address was meant to give Americans hope.

ABRAHAM LINCOLN

Abraham Lincoln grew up poor. He lived on different farms throughout his childhood. He did not receive much schooling, but learned to love reading. Lincoln went on to become the 16th US president in 1861. He helped keep the Union states together during the US Civil War. Lincoln also helped end slavery. His work made him one of the most important presidents in US history. Visitors can now stop at the Lincoln Memorial when visiting Washington, DC.

Lincoln paid tribute to the fallen soldiers with his speech.

UNKNOWN

U.S. SOLDIER

Who Wrote the Gettysburg Address?

Lincoln wrote the Gettysburg Address himself. He was one of the few presidents in history believed to have written all his speeches. However, the timeline of when he wrote the speech is a matter of some dispute. Some historians believe it was written in the weeks leading up to the event. Others believe he wrote the speech during his train ride to Gettysburg. Another theory is that Lincoln wrote it the evening before. Notes of the speech have not been found. No one knows the true story.

Lincoln wrote the Gettysburg Address by hand, though it's not clear where or when he wrote it.

Judge Wills reportedly told the *Philadelphia Inquirer* in early October that Lincoln was expected to be at the event. This would have given Lincoln more than a month to prepare his speech. Many historians believe Lincoln would have started taking notes right away.

Lincoln took a train to Gettysburg a few days before the dedication

14
Length, in inches (36 cm), of the paper Lincoln used to draft the address.

- Lincoln wrote the Gettysburg Address himself.
- There are many theories regarding when Lincoln wrote the speech.
- Lincoln may have known in early October about the event.
- There are accounts from people who saw Lincoln writing during his train ride and on the night before the event.

ceremony. Several other important figures and members of the press also rode the train. Lincoln left the group during part of the trip. He was in his private car. Many thought he was working on his speech. It is also possible he wrote part or all of the speech the night before the ceremony. Lincoln was invited to stay at Wills's home. Wills claims to have seen Lincoln writing in his room late at night.

Lincoln had a gift with words, both written and in public speaking.

4

When Was the Gettysburg Address Delivered?

The dedication of the Gettysburg National Cemetery took place on November 19, 1863. It was an afternoon filled with prayer, music, and multiple speakers. A chaplain prayed over the graves of the soldiers who were killed in the recent Battle of Gettysburg. Then the Marine Band played a few hymns. Next was the main event of the ceremony. Everett was one of the greatest speakers of the 1800s. He had worked as a professor, congressman, governor, and senator. Everett had even run against Lincoln in the 1860 presidential election. People were looking forward to hearing him speak.

Identical white stones mark the soldiers' graves at the Gettysburg National Cemetery.

They traveled from many states for this event.

Everett spoke for two hours. This was common for well-known speakers at the time. Everett spoke about the Battle of Gettysburg and its meaning. He tried to focus his speech on the future. Everett thought this would be one of the greatest speeches of his life. He did not know the speech following his would be discussed for years to come.

Lincoln took the stage after Everett was done speaking. He only spoke for a short period of time. But his words had a large impact. The crowd had mostly been silent throughout the day out of respect. Lincoln spoke from the heart. His words gave the crowd hope for the future of the country.

13,607
Number of words in Everett's speech.

- The dedication ceremony took place on the afternoon of November 19, 1863.
- Everett was the main speaker of the event.
- People traveled from near and far to hear Everett speak.
- Lincoln's address was very short in comparison to Everett's speech.

A memorial was placed near the site where Lincoln delivered his famous speech.

LINCOLN ADDRESS MEMORIAL
This monument commemorates Lincoln's Gettysburg Address, November 19, 1863.
The Address was delivered about 300 yards from this spot along the upper Cemetery drive. The site is now marked by the Soldiers' National Monument.
Dedicated Jan. 24, 1912 - Sculptor, Henry Bush-Brown

Why Was Lincoln Asked to Speak at Gettysburg?

Lincoln began his presidency in 1861. He took a strong stand against slavery. His position on this issue contributed to the start of the US Civil War. Thousands of Union soldiers needed to be buried after the Battle of Gettysburg. The dedication ceremony on November 19 would be a way to honor these soldiers.

The cemetery in Gettysburg would be a national monument. As is the case today, important figures, including the president, were invited to dedication ceremonies of national monuments. Lincoln was invited by Judge Wills to attend the Gettysburg National Cemetery dedication. The governors of the Union states also requested that Lincoln attend. They

Lincoln often visited Union troops on the battlefield during the war.

hoped the leader of the United States would deliver a few remarks. Lincoln would only be a small part of the ceremony. But it was important he attended to honor the soldiers who were killed in battle.

- The dedication ceremony on November 19 would honor the Union soldiers.
- The cemetery at Gettysburg would be a national monument.
- Important figures, including the president, generally attend national monument dedications.
- The governors of the Union states requested that Lincoln deliver a few remarks.

Lincoln met with Union generals, including Ulysses S. Grant (far right), to get updates on the war.

6

What Does the Gettysburg Address Say?

As commander in chief during one of the country's bloodiest conflicts, Lincoln needed to give meaning to the US Civil War. He needed to explain why the war was necessary for the good of the country. Lincoln also needed to bring peace to grieving families. His Gettysburg Address attempted to do just that.

Lincoln reminded the crowd that the country was founded on equality with his opening lines: "Four score and seven years ago our fathers brought forth . . . the proposition that all men are created equal." Lincoln honored the Union soldiers who had given their lives for freedom. But he also noted that it was the job of

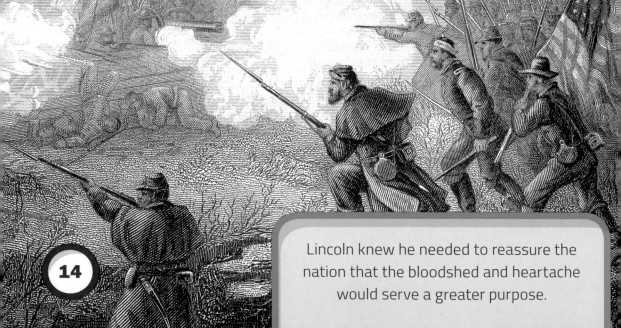

Lincoln knew he needed to reassure the nation that the bloodshed and heartache would serve a greater purpose.

20

Number of years in a "score" as referenced in the Gettysburg Address.

- The Gettysburg Address would give meaning to the US Civil War.
- Lincoln reminded the crowd that the country was founded on equality.
- He honored the Union soldiers for giving their lives for freedom.
- The Gettysburg Address described how the war was a fight for equality.

CHANGING TIMES

Many speeches in the 1800s were fancy and used big phrases and words. The speeches could be difficult to understand. Speakers also were known to talk for hours at a time. This was the speaking style Everett used at the dedication. But the world of communication was changing at the time. People were typing out quick, direct messages on telegraphs. Lincoln recognized this change. He used simpler and more concise language for his Gettysburg Address.

those who survived the war to continue to defend democracy and freedom.

Lincoln's speech became a defining moment for citizens of the Union. It changed how they viewed freedom and government. Lincoln ended his speech by saying that "government of the people, by the people, for the people, shall not perish from the earth." Before the Gettysburg Address, people assumed the war was only about ending slavery. Now, it became clear that it was a fight for equality for all people.

The 4th Ohio Infantry Monument overlooks the battlefield from Cemetery Hill.

Where Did the Ideas in the Address Come From?

Lincoln loved to read. It is no surprise, then, that he pulled thoughts and ideas from other places to use in his speeches. The Gettysburg Address was no different. Many of the ideas Lincoln referred to in his speech were not new. Authors, Supreme Court justices, reverends, and important government documents inspired him as he wrote the Gettysburg Address.

Senator Daniel Webster made a statement several years earlier regarding the government and where its power comes from. He noted that the Constitution and the government were made by and for the people. Supreme Court Justice John

Marshall had agreed, saying that the people had the power to benefit themselves. In 1858, a reverend gave a similar speech in Boston, Massachusetts. Lincoln had even said similar words to Congress in

Webster was a successful courtroom attorney and US senator from Massachusetts.

87

Number of years prior to the Gettysburg Address that the Declaration of Independence was written.

- Lincoln pulled ideas from other places to use in the Gettysburg Address.
- The idea that the government got its power from the people was a common theme in the address.
- Lincoln built on this idea and created an inspirational speech for Americans.
- The Declaration of Independence was also a main source for Lincoln's speech.

IN CONGRESS, JULY 4, 1776.

The unanimous Declaration of the thirteen united States of America.

Famous documents, such as the Declaration of Independence, influenced Lincoln's speech.

July 1861. Lincoln built on this theme to inspire his audience.

Lincoln also relied heavily on the Declaration of Independence for his speech. Many people believed the Constitution was the founding document of the United States. But in his Gettysburg Address, Lincoln claims it was the Declaration. This was the document that talked about equality for all.

What Does Lincoln Refer to in the Address?

Lincoln wanted to honor the Union soldiers who had died in the Battle of Gettysburg. But he also wanted his speech to be more than that. Rather than focus on details of the US Civil War, Lincoln wanted to talk about bigger ideals. In his speech, Lincoln left out some common words heard at the time. *Gettysburg*, *slavery*, *Union*, and *Confederate* were absent from the Gettysburg Address.

Instead, Lincoln discussed loyalty, democracy, equality, and honor. He talked about the unfinished work Americans had after the deaths of the soldiers. Lincoln also noted

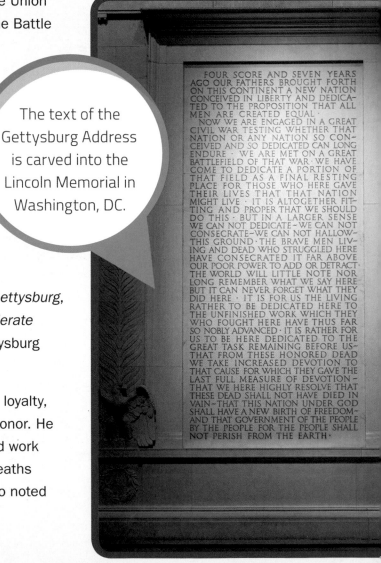

The text of the Gettysburg Address is carved into the Lincoln Memorial in Washington, DC.

The Lincoln Memorial is one of the most popular attractions in the nation's capital.

that Americans needed to work to achieve freedom. They could not have a government of the people without equality. Lincoln also was speaking to the entire world in his speech, rather than just the United States. By not referencing the war, the Gettysburg Address became timeless. Lincoln's words are still relevant years later.

272
Number of words in the Gettysburg Address.

- Lincoln wanted the Gettysburg Address to be about more than war details.
- He did not use the words *Gettysburg, slavery, Union*, or *Confederate*.
- Lincoln focused on bigger ideals such as loyalty, democracy, equality, and honor.
- This has made the Gettysburg Address timeless.

Who Was the Audience of the Gettysburg Address?

After the deadly Battle of Gettysburg, Union soldiers and leaders knew a national cemetery was needed. This space would honor those soldiers who had died fighting for a united country. Judge Wills planned the dedication ceremony for November 19.

Along with the 2,000 residents of the growing town of Gettysburg, thousands more people traveled to Pennsylvania for the event. Union soldiers attended the dedication. They lined the streets leading to the cemetery. They also formed lines surrounding the main stage. Families of current and deceased soldiers were there, including children. Important government officials and leaders also attended. Governors, Cabinet members, and military officers sat on the main stage.

Lincoln addressing the crowd at Gettysburg

Lincoln also sat there next to Everett and the other speakers. The night before the ceremony, Lincoln and 37 other public figures stayed at Judge Wills's home.

Members of the media were also at the dedication ceremony. These included newspaper writers and photographers. However, without modern sound equipment, it was hard for some reporters to hear all of the speakers.

Union soldiers were among the crowd gathered for the dedication.

15,000
Estimated number of people attending the dedication ceremony.

- The town of Gettysburg had a population of 2,000 people.
- Union soldiers lined the streets leading to the cemetery.
- Men, women, and children were in attendance.
- Important government officials sat on the main stage, including the president, governors, Cabinet members, and military officers.

NEWSPAPER ACCOUNTS

Newspaper writers attended the Gettysburg National Cemetery dedication. Microphones and recording tools had not yet been invented. The writers tried to write down what they heard, word by word. This led to several errors. Some of the writers were able to see a copy of Lincoln's speech after he spoke. That helped correct any errors. Still, historians have a hard time relying on the accuracy of these newspaper accounts.

21

How Did People React to the Gettysburg Address?

After Lincoln finished speaking on November 19, the reaction was mixed. Lincoln's speech was much shorter than Everett's. The audience did not respond immediately, not knowing whether he would continue speaking. Lincoln was worried that his speech had not made the impact he hoped for. However, in the days to come, reactions both critical and supportive rolled in.

Many newspapers across the North reprinted Lincoln's speech the following day. The newspapers and people who did not support the president were critical of his speech. They called it "silly" and "shameful." The *Harrisburg Patriot and Union* even went as far as saying Lincoln's words would never be repeated or thought of again.

The Gettysburg Solemnities.

DEDICATION

OF

The National Cemetery

AT

GETTYSBURG, PENNSYLVANIA,

NOVEMBER 19, 1863.

WITH THE

ORATION OF HON. EDWARD EVERETT

SPEECH OF PRESIDENT LINCOLN,

&c., &c., &c.

This pamphlet, printed days after the dedication, contains the full text of Everett's and Lincoln's addresses.

PUBLISHED AT THE WASHINGTON CHRONICLE OFFICE.

4

Number of known newspaper copyists working in Gettysburg the day of the event.

- Lincoln worried his speech had little impact when the audience was slow to respond.
- One newspaper said Lincoln's Gettysburg Address would be forgotten and never repeated.
- Other people praised Lincoln's speech, saying it was beautiful and from the heart.

THINK ABOUT IT

Why do you think some people did not like Lincoln's address? Use information from this book and another source to support your answer.

Although the speech was criticized, it quickly became celebrated. People even began to quote the address. Everett quickly wrote to Lincoln praising him for such a strong and short speech. The *Springfield Republican* noted that Lincoln's speech would be long admired by people. *Harper's Weekly* said Lincoln's words came from the heart and were emotional. The *Providence Journal* called the speech admirable and beautiful.

A plaque indicates the pew where Lincoln sat at a church service held after the dedication.

11

How Many Versions of the Address Are There?

Historians over the years have had a hard time determining the exact wording of the Gettysburg Address. Although it was a short speech, there are five known copies of the address in Lincoln's handwriting. Some historians argue that each of the copies differs slightly from what Lincoln said that day. Each of the five copies is named after the person who received it.

Two of the copies of the address were written before Lincoln delivered the speech. Lincoln gave these copies to his two private secretaries, John Nicolay and John Hay. Both men were at Gettysburg with Lincoln. The Nicolay copy is considered by many people to be the first copy. It begins on White House stationery and then is finished on a different type of paper. The Hay copy has handwritten changes on it.

Three more copies of the speech were written after the ceremony and

A reproduction of the Gettysburg Address

Address delivered
Cemetery at Gettysb

Four score and seven years ago our fathers brought forth on this continent, a new na= tion, conceived in Liberty, and dedicated to the proposition that all men are cre= ted equal.
...ced in a great civil war,
...any nation

The Lincoln Bedroom at the White House has been restored with furnishings from the era.

given as mementos or gifts. The Everett copy was written for Edward Everett in 1864. This copy is now at the Illinois State Historical Library in Springfield, Illinois. Historian George Bancroft also requested a copy of the speech. The Bancroft copy is now at Cornell University in New York. The fifth copy of the speech was made for Colonel Alexander Bliss. Bliss was Bancroft's stepson. This copy is now on display in the Lincoln Bedroom at the White House.

THE BLISS COPY

Bancroft was putting together a book to raise money for soldiers. He wanted to include Lincoln's words in his own handwriting. However, Lincoln wrote that version on both sides of the paper. Due to the technological limitations of the time, that made it impossible to copy. Bancroft's stepson, Colonel Bliss, asked Lincoln to make another copy for the book. This is the last known copy written by Lincoln. It is also the only copy Lincoln signed and dated. This is the version that is most commonly reprinted.

What Was the Impact of the Gettysburg Address?

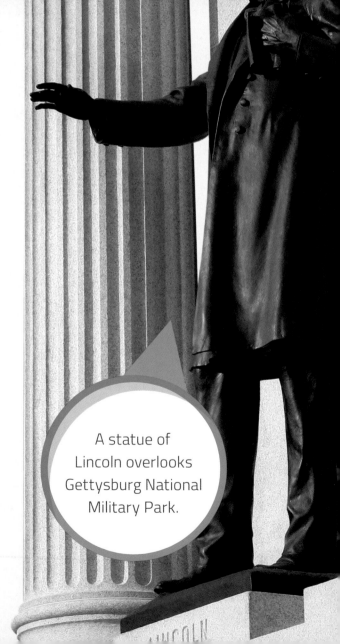

Thousands of people attended the dedication of the Gettysburg National Cemetery. Although immediately following the event there were mixed opinions about Lincoln's address, his words eventually became a world-famous speech. But it would take time to reach this level.

Lincoln's speech was comforting for the people affected by the battles of the US Civil War. He honored the soldiers who had died. Lincoln also inspired Northerners. He made it clear that the United States would move forward after the war. The people appreciated Lincoln's words, but they quickly forgot his message. It was not until 1877, long after Lincoln's death, when a railroad company encouraged tourists to visit the Gettysburg

A statue of Lincoln overlooks Gettysburg National Military Park.

14

Number of years that passed before tourists were encouraged to visit Gettysburg.

- There were mixed opinions about Lincoln's speech before it was considered famous.
- Lincoln's speech was comforting and inspiring for Americans but quickly forgotten.
- A railroad company advertisement was the first to call Lincoln's speech memorable.
- The constitution of France uses some of Lincoln's words from the Gettysburg Address.

THINK ABOUT IT

With an adult's help, find another speech that references Lincoln's Gettysburg Address. What is the speech about? Why do you think the author chose the Gettysburg Address for inspiration?

and documents referenced it. Before delivering his "I Have a Dream" speech, Dr. Martin Luther King Jr. said he wanted his speech to be similar to the Gettysburg Address. The constitution of France uses some words from the address. And the first president of China said he was inspired by Lincoln's words when writing an important document.

National Cemetery. The company's advertisement stated this was where Lincoln's "immortal speech" was delivered. One year later, President Rutherford Hayes also called Lincoln's speech memorable. Lincoln's speech slowly became more famous.

Lincoln's Gettysburg Address became so famous that other important speeches

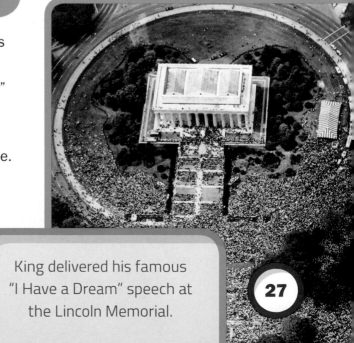

King delivered his famous "I Have a Dream" speech at the Lincoln Memorial.

Fact Sheet

- The Library of Congress had special cases built for the two copies of the Gettysburg Address that it owns. These cases have stainless steel frames with clear panels. They allow people to see the documents from both sides of the cases. Inside the cases is a special gas that replaces all the oxygen. This keeps the correct moisture level for the documents. The Library of Congress also has a low-temperature vault where these cases are stored. Other important documents are kept in this vault as well.

- Lincoln's speech was so short that there are no pictures of him speaking at the dedication. The official photographer of the event spent most of his time photographing Everett. After Everett was finished speaking, the photographer had to set up his camera again. Lincoln was done before the photographer finished his setup.

- There were too many new burials in Gettysburg National Cemetery the day of the dedication for the speeches to be held there. The main stage was set up in a nearby cemetery.

- The Gettysburg Address copy at the White House is usually on display in the Lincoln Bedroom. It is on the second floor of the White House. This room was Lincoln's office and cabinet room. President Harry S. Truman named it the Lincoln Bedroom in 1945.

- On July 4, 1865, the Soldiers' National Monument cornerstone was laid in Gettysburg National Cemetery. It is a monument in the center of the graves. The four angles of the monument represent war, history, peace, and plenty.

Glossary

address
A formal speech.

ceremony
A formal event that is part of a social occasion.

copyists
People who made written copies of documents.

dedication
A ceremony to mark the opening of something.

hymns
Religious songs.

industries
Businesses that provide certain products or services.

keynote
The main theme of an event.

plantations
Large areas of land in hotter climates where crops are grown.

territories
Areas of land that belong to the government.

For More Information

Books

Ford, Carin T. *Lincoln's Gettysburg Address and the Battle of Gettysburg through Primary Sources.* Berkeley Heights, NJ: Enslow, 2013.

George, Enzo. *The Civil War.* New York: Cavendish Square Publishing, 2015.

Gregory, Josh. *The Gettysburg Address.* New York: Children's Press, 2013.

O'Connor, Jim. *What Was the Battle of Gettysburg?* New York: Grosset & Dunlap, 2013.

Visit 12StoryLibrary.com

Scan the code or use your school's login at **12StoryLibrary.com** for recent updates about this topic and a full digital version of this book. Enjoy free access to:

- Digital ebook
- Breaking news updates
- Live content feeds
- Videos, interactive maps, and graphics
- Additional web resources

Note to educators: Visit 12StoryLibrary.com/register to sign up for free premium website access. Enjoy live content plus a full digital version of every 12-Story Library book you own for every student at your school.

Index

About the Author

Mirella S. Miller is the author and editor of several children's books. She lives in Minnesota with her husband and their dog.